Chapter One

The World of Big Cats

Lions, **tigers**, **leopards**, **cheetahs**, and **jaguars** are big cats. They're a lot like small cats. But big cats are much bigger. And most big cats do not purr. They roar! *GRRR!*

All cats belong to the same family. Big and small cats have almost 250 bones in their bodies. That's about 40 more bones than you have. The extra bones let cats twist and bend freely.

Super-sharp eyes help make cats good hunters. By day, they see about as well as you do. But at night they see much better.

Cats have a special layer in the back of their eyes. It lets them see in very dim light. The layer also makes their eyes shine in the dark.

Thirty sharp, pointed teeth help cats grab and hold the animals they hunt. These animals are called **prey.**

Every cat has five curved claws on each front paw. Each back paw has four claws. Most cats pull their claws in when they are not using them. This keeps the claws very sharp.

Did you know that cats are great sleepers? Some rest up to 18 hours each day. While asleep, big cats keep their tails straight out. Small cats curl their tails around their bodies.

All cats sleep lightly. Some even doze with one eye partly open.

Chapter Two

Lions: The Loudest

Of all the big cats, **lions** roar the loudest. *GRRR!* But they do not roar to frighten prey. Roaring helps them keep in touch with each other. It also helps lions warn other lions to stay away.

Lions are very strong and powerful. One healthy adult lion can drag a full-grown zebra along the ground. It would take six husky men to do the same!

Most lions live in Africa. A few smaller ones live in North and South America.

African lions make their homes on open, grassy plains. There they can find lots of prey to catch and eat.

Lions have brownish yellow fur that is the color of dry grass. The color helps lions to hide while they hunt. Lions mostly prey on zebras, antelopes, wild pigs, and even water buffalo.

The male lion has a big collar of long, thick hair called a **mane**. The mane makes the lion look larger than he is.

The mane also protects the lion's neck from the bites of other male lions and enemies.

A female lion is called a **lioness**. A lioness is usually smaller and lighter than a male lion. Yet, the females do most of the hunting.

The hungry lioness hunts in a special way. She holds her body low and close to the ground. Quietly, she creeps toward her prey. When near, the lioness leaps forward. She seizes the prey with her teeth and flings it to the ground. Then she bites its neck.

The lioness drags the dead prey to a shady spot. But she does not eat it right away. She waits until the males gather. They feed first.

The lions rip off chunks of meat.
GULP! GULP! They swallow huge pieces
without chewing. One lion can eat as much
as 75 pounds of food at a single feeding!

Do you think lions eat three meals a
day the way you do? The answer is no.
Lions usually feed just once every three or
four days. It's no wonder they eat so much
at a time.

A lion and a lioness pair off and breed when they are about three or four years old. The young lions are called **cubs**.

At first, the cubs can't see or walk. But the lioness takes good care of them. For over a month she feeds them milk from her body.

The mother hides her babies in safe spots. From time to time, she changes hiding places. She carries the helpless cubs in her mouth, one at a time. After a month, she brings her cubs their first taste of meat.

Lions are the only big cats that live in groups. These groups are called **prides**. A pride can have up to 35 males, females, and cubs.

While the lions and lionesses hunt, the cubs play games and wrestle. They learn to hunt by watching the adults. The rest of the time, they sleep or rest. *Shh.*

Chapter Three

Tigers: The Largest

Tigers are the largest of the big cats. Each fully grown tiger is about nine feet long. It can weigh over 500 pounds. Imagine an animal longer and heavier than a sofa!

Tigers live in Asia. Most lions, you know, live in Africa. So lions and tigers almost never meet—except in zoos.

You can find tigers in different parts of Asia. In the south, Indian tigers live in hot tropical rain forests. The larger Siberian tigers roam the cold forests of the north. Still other tigers make their homes in swamps and wetlands.

Tigers seem to enjoy water more than the other big cats. In fact, they often jump into water the way kids do at a pool.

Tigers are great swimmers. Sometimes they swim across wide rivers to find prey.

Or, they hunt for food in the water. But on hot, sunny days tigers might not fish at all. They might just paddle in the water to keep cool.

Like other big cats, tigers catch prey with their teeth and claws. Tigers hunt the same animals as lions do. But tigers also eat fish, turtles, frogs, porcupines, and monkeys.

The tiger's coat is brownish yellow to orange. Most striking are its dark black stripes. The stripes help to hide the tiger among trees and tall grass. Every tiger has its own pattern of stripes. You will never see two patterns that are alike.

Tigers mostly hunt at night. They search out old, very young, or injured animals. That's because weak prey are easier to catch than healthy animals. But hunting weak prey is not as easy as you may think. Tigers are able to kill only about one out of every ten animals they attack.

A tiger charges its prey from behind. It knocks the animal to the ground. Then the tiger bites the neck to make the kill.

Before eating, the tiger drags its victim to a safe hiding place. This hiding spot can be behind rocks or trees or in tall grass. Mos often, it is near water.

Here the tiger eats its meal. It tears off and swallows huge hunks of meat. The tiger leaves only the animal's bones and stomach. Then the tiger takes a big drink of water—an lies down for a nice, long nap.

One tiger eats about 50 large animals in a year. A mother tiger with cubs eats even more—up to 70 animals a year! It needs the extra food to feed its hungry cubs.

Long ago there were lots of tigers in Asia. But human hunters killed many of them. Also, people built farms, houses, and roads on tiger territory. The tigers had few places to live and hunt. More tigers died.

Today there are fewer than 5,000 tigers left in the wild. Some people protect tigers in large parks. Others try to save tigers in zoos. Even so, tigers are in danger of disappearing forever.

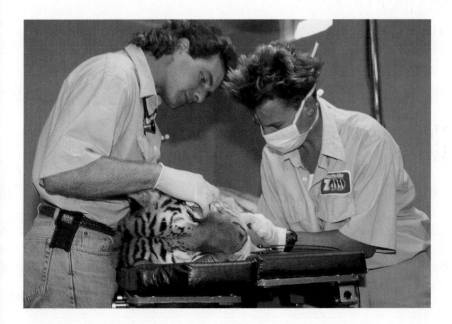

Leopards:
The Best Climbers

Leopards make their homes in Africa and Asia. They hunt mainly in forests. Excellent climbers, leopards live both on the ground and in trees.

The coats of most leopards are light tan with black spots. The spots make the leopards hard to see when the sun shines through the branches of trees.

This helps hide them from their prey. It also keeps them safe from enemy attacks.

One kind of leopard is the snow leopard. It lives high in the mountains of Asia. Its thick coat is light gray with brown spots. A light-colored coat is good for hiding in snow.

Leopards that are big and black are  sometimes called **panthers**. Panthers have black spots on black fur. Very few panthers are left in the wild.

Leopards prey on large animals, such as antelopes, gazelles, zebras, sheep, and goats. They also hunt lion and cheetah cubs.

After making a kill, the leopard carries its prey up a tree. The leopard puts the animal on a branch and starts to feed. Other animals want to share the meal. But none can climb as well as the leopard.

The leopard feeds slowly. After a while it stops eating. Usually, there is still plenty of m left on the bones. But the leopard leaves it to another time. For now, the leopard stretches on a sturdy tree branch to rest or sleep.

Leopards roar mostly when fighting one another. Otherwise, they bark or cough. In leopard "talk" a bark means, "Look out!" A number of barks in a row warn other leopards to keep away.

Leopards in tropical areas have babies all year round. In cooler areas, leopards bear their cubs only in the spring.

The mother leopard usually gives birth in a hole in the ground, in a clump of bushes, or in a hollow tree trunk. Most litters contain two or three cubs.

The newborn cubs cannot see. Their eyes are tightly shut. In about one week the eyes open.

For the first three months the cubs drink their mother's milk. After that, the mother teaches them how to find food. At a year or so, the cubs are ready to hunt for themselves.

Chapter Five

Cheetahs: The Fastest

Cheetahs are smaller than the other big cats. But they can run much faster. In fact, the cheetah is the fastest of all land animals. With its long legs and slim body, it reaches speeds of 70 miles per hour! That's faster than the cars on a highway!

Most cheetahs live in Africa.
At birth, young cheetahs are the size
of kittens. The mother hides them from
hyenas. Hyenas will attack cheetah cubs
that are left alone. A mother stays close to
her cubs until they are grown.

Like leopards, cheetahs are brownish yellow with black spots. But cheetahs have two dark stripes that run from their eyes to their mouth. This is a good way to tell cheetahs from leopards.

Cheetahs are unlike the other big cats in two important ways. Cheetahs do not roar. Nor can they pull in their claws like lions, tigers, leopards, or jaguars. The claws are always out and ready to use. They grip the ground as the cheetahs race along.

Cheetahs can run very fast for only a short while. They easily get out of breath. If they do not catch their prey right away, they give up and rest.

Just like any other big cat, a hungry cheetah looks for prey. But a cheetah does not pounce on its victim. Instead, it chases the prey. Then a quick bite usually kills the animal.

A cheetah eats its prey very quickly. But it rarely cleans all the meat off the bones. Jackals and vultures wait until the cheetah goes away. Then they feast on the leftovers.

Jaguars: The Strongest

The **jaguar** looks like a leopard. But its spots are different. Many of the spots are rings with black dots in the middle. A leopard's spots do not have dots.

The jaguar is slightly larger than a leopard. It also has a shorter tail. And it is a more powerful animal.

The jaguar is the strongest big cat in Central and South America. It rules the jungles in this part of the world.

No other animal will fight a jaguar. But jaguars sometimes fight each other. This mostly happens when one jaguar tries to steal another jaguar's prey.

Until the 1900s jaguars even lived in the United States! But hunters shot many of them. Now no jaguars live in the United States or Canada.

Jaguars are forest hunters, just like leopards. What's more, they are also good climbers that often hide in trees.

Like tigers, jaguars are not afraid of water and will swim across wide rivers. Sometimes they catch fish there.

On land, jaguars hunt large animals, such as deer and wild pigs. Hungry jaguars also prey on small animals, such as turtles and lizards. All big cats are great hunters. But sad to say, they are also widely hunted. Thus big cats are becoming very rare.

So let us remember to:
- respect lions, tigers, leopards, cheetahs, and jaguars,
- get to know them better, and
- work to save them!

Index

Berger Science Readers

GRRR!

A Book About
BIG CATS

by Melvin & Gilda Berger

SCHOLASTIC INC.

New York Toronto London Auckland Sydney
Mexico City New Delhi Hong Kong Buenos Aires

For Elizabeth, cat lover extraordinaire!
— M.B. and G.B.

Special thanks to Paul Sieswerda
of The Wildlife Conservation Society
for his expertise

Photography credits:

Cover: Guido Alberto Rossi/The Image Bank/Getty Images; page 3 and pages 18-19: Tom & Pat Leeson/Photo Researchers; pages 4-5: Francois Gohier/ Photo Researchers; page 6: Muriel Nicolotti-Bios/Peter Arnold, Inc.; page 7: Fritz Polking/Peter Arnold, Inc.; pages 8-9: N.O. Tomalin/Bruce Coleman Inc.; pages 10-11: Ed Degginger/Bruce Coleman Inc.; page 12: K. Ammann/Bruce Coleman Inc.; page 13: Paul Funston/Photo Researchers; pages 14-15: Joe McDonald/ Bruce Coleman Inc.; page 14 bottom: Gregory G. Dinijian/Photo Researchers; page 16 top: Martin W. Grosnick/Bruce Coleman Inc.; page 16 bottom: Lorne Sulcas/Peter Arnold, Inc.; page 17 bottom: Norman Owen Tomalin/Bruce Coleman Inc.; page 17 top: Ted Kerasote/Photo Researchers; page 20: Tom Brakefield/Bruce Coleman Inc.; page 21: Erwin and Peggy Bauer/Bruce Coleman Inc.; pages 22-23: Renee Lynn/Photo Researchers; page 25: Tom Brakefield/ Bruce Coleman Inc.; pages 26-27: Anup Shah/Dembinsky Photo Associates; page 28 top: Tom Brakefield/ Bruce Coleman Inc.; page 28 bottom: Mark Newman/Photo Researchers; page 29: Anup Shah/Dembinsky Photo Associates; page 30: Manfred Danegger/Peter Arnold, Inc.; page 31: Alan & Sandy Carey/Photo Researchers; pages 32-33: F. Polking/Peter Arnold, Inc.; page 34: Mark Newman/Photo Researchers; page 35: Tim Davis/Photo Researchers; pages 36-37: Erwin and Peggy Bauer/Bruce Coleman Inc.; page 38: Tom & Pat Leeson/Photo Researchers; page 39: Tom Brakefield/Bruce Coleman Inc.

ISBN 0-439-80182-6

12 11 10 9 8 7 6 5 4 3 2 1   5 6 7 8 9 10/0

Printed in the U.S.A.
First revised edition, September 2005

...erger Science Readers

GRRR!

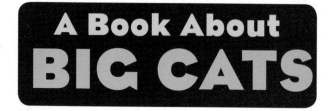

A Book About
BIG CATS